Burnt Sienna

Copyright © 2020, 2017 Joshua Bohnsack

Published by Long Day Press
Chicago, Il 60647
LongDayPress.com
@LongDayPress

All rights reserved. No part of this book may be reproduced for any reason or by any means without written permission excepting brief passages for reviewing purposes. Please don't steal from us.

ISBN 9781950987122 (Paperback Edition)
ISBN 9781087914374 (eBook Edition)
Library of Congress Control Number: 2020946883

Edited by Joseph Demes

Acknowledgements:

An unbound, limited edition of *Burnt Sienna* was published by Throwback Books in 2017.

The following stories were previously published: "Boilermaker" published as "Qualified," in *5x5*; "Unnatural Light" published as "Days," in *Centrifuge*; "Golden Cadillac," published as "Aging," in *BRILLIANT Flash Fiction*; "Bronx," in *Vanilla Sex Magazine*; "Jon Collins," in *Rejection Letters*; "Whiskey Sour," in *Sporklet*.

Printed in the United States of America
Second Edition

Burnt Sienna

Cocktails & Stories

Joshua Bohnsack

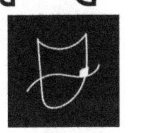

Long Day Press
Chicago

Contents

Jon Collins	1
Bronx	3
White Grape Blossom	5
Irish Coffee	7
Unnatural Light	9
Supernova	11
[when you have forgotten] Sunday Morning	13
Golden Cadillac	15
Boilermaker	17
Colorado Bulldog	19
Whiskey Sour	21
Rob Roy	23
Vodka Redbull	25
Gin Blossom	29

Jon Collins

Ingredients:
- ¼ oz lemon juice
- 1 oz simple syrup
- Soda water
- 2 oz whiskey

Preparation:
- Mix lemon juice and simple syrup in a Collins glass with soda water.
- Shake in a tumbler and pour back into Collins glass.
- Top with 2 oz whiskey for layered effect.
- Garnish with a lemon slice.

You came to the bar and said, make me something. I asked if you like whiskey.

You said, not really.

I said, too bad.

You drank the cocktail and said you'd had a bad night.

I said, I'm sorry, and you asked, why are you sorry, and I said, I guess I don't know.

Bronx

Ingredients:
- 1½ oz Tanqueray Gin
- 1 oz Fresh-squeezed orange juice
- ½ oz sweet vermouth
- ½ oz dry vermouth

Preparation:
- Mix and shake in cocktail shaker.
- Serve up in chilled glass with an orange twist.

The other bartender didn't know what it was, nor did you. It was something they drank in *This Side of Paradise*. You looked up the recipe, handed him your phone.

You needed a drink. You needed a break. You hated that book. White males, Ivy League school, running through women like they own them. The only strong female runs her horse off a cliff. No Zelda. What a way to try to go out.

He slid your drink across the bar. He handed you back the phone with his contact information pulled up.

"I'm off around 3."

You held the martini glass with a full fist. You drank the cocktail without breaking his eye contact. You grabbed your coat, threw down a $20, and walked home.

White Grape Blossom

Ingredients:
- 1½ oz Effen Cucumber Vodka
- 1 oz St. Germain Elderflower Liqueur
- 1½ oz sweet & sour mix
- ½ oz simple syrup
- 6 white grapes, more for garnish
- Basil, real fresh floral basil

Preparation:
- In cocktail shaker, muddle 6 white grapes and about 5 basil leaves with a splash of simple syrup.
- Fill shaker halfway with ice, combine vodka, Saint Germaine, and sweet & sour, shake and serve up in chilled martini glass.
- Garnish with grapes and a basil leaf. Wrap the basil leaf around a grape before skewering to add a delicate cradling effect.

Work was slow and I spent forty-eight minutes trying to order you flowers through my iPhone, because I thought it would cheer you up, but the order wouldn't process, because my card kept getting declined, so I called the florist and to explain to them that I only had nineteen dollars in my account and to see if they would shed some mercy on me, but they said they couldn't, so I called my mom and told her what had happened and she ended up giving me her credit card number, so really, it's her you should thank.

Irish Coffee

Ingredients:
- 1½ oz Paddy Irish Whiskey
- 1 oz Ryan's Irish Cream Liqueur

Preparation:
- Top with dark roast coffee; the more grounds, the better.
- Serve in an off white or eggshell colored mug.

He spilled his coffee, immersing the box scores of the sports section. You were his server and hurried with a rag and the dark rimmed pot. He absorbed the stream running off the edge of the table, before it reached the vinyl booth and, inevitably, his khakis.

With one hand, you poured the remains of the batch into his speckled mug, your other hand rested on his seat back, so close to his shoulder.

You told him, "I left room. I hope you have more in your flask."

Unnatural Light

Ingredients:
- 1 case of Natty Light
- 1 large red Igloo cooler
- 2 small bags of ice
- 1 record-breaking heat wave in the midst of a Midwestern July

Preparation:
- Layer cooler with 1 small bag of ice, 1 case of Natty Light, then 1 small bag of ice.
- Let sit and try to get some work done until you can't take it anymore.

When I was a kid, I asked my dad how many beers it took to get him drunk.

He told me, "On days like today, a million."

Supernova

Ingredients:
- 1 oz Fireball Whiskey
- ½ oz orange juice

Preparation:
- Mix ingredients in cocktail shaker with ice.
- Shake and distribute into shot glasses.
- Add splash of grenadine for layered effect.
- Go out with a bang.

Note: Makes one shot.

Do you remember that time you were driving us to The Lion's Club Park to donate blood, and we saw the aftermath of a car crash where a student driver had been t-boned by a pickup truck and I said my old drivers' ed teacher was in the front seat and you asked me his blood type?

[when you have forgotten] Sunday Morning

Ingredients:
- 1½ oz cheap Scotch
- 1½ oz amaro
- ¾ oz lime juice
- Ginger beer

Preparation:
- Combine Scotch, Amaro, and lime juice in shaker with ice.
- Pour into a Collins glass and add ginger beer.
- Garnish with a lime.

You wrote 'i love you' first on a coaster I took from a pub in Dublin the same day Lou Reed died. I tried to take work off, because I was in mourning, but my boss said "no," and I played *The Velvet Underground & Nico* on repeat all night until a drunk at the bar asked me to play Steppenwolf.

Golden Cadillac

Ingredients:

- 1½ oz Galliano herbal liqueur
- 2 oz crème de cacao
- 3 full scoops of vanilla ice cream

Preparation:

- Mix ingredients in a blender to a desired texture.
- Serve up in a rocks glass with a straw and spoon.

Working in the shop, with all these seventy-something, degenerating people eating their large twist cones at 2 in the afternoon, makes me worry about my own mortality, like when two elderly customers know each other and make small talk, I start to wonder if we'll grow up, then fifty years later, I'll be waiting for some teenager to make me a large twist cone and you'll walk through the door, just as my wrinkled palm grasps the cake cone, I notice your cane, and try to gaze into your eyes to see if they are the same shade of hazel, but can't really tell, because you're wearing those big, dark sunglasses that cover your eyeglasses as you drive, and I'll recall how nearsighted you were when we met and wonder if you got that semi-corrective surgery, which technically hasn't been invented yet, because this scenario is fifty years in the future, and your auburn hair is filled with so many strands of silver and mine has been turning gray since I was 19, so the color on my head had long since passed, and we'll stop for a second and exchange "hellos" and "how-about-this-weathers" on our climate-changed planet and I'll try to straighten my spine against gravity, because you always said I was too short, and I'll ask if you still hate tomatoes and I hope you say yes, but I know we will be in different towns and I'll be wishing for this the next fifty years.

Boilermaker

Ingredients:
- Toppling Goliath's Dorothy's New World Lager
- 1 ½ oz Cedar Ridge Iowa Bourbon Whiskey

Preparation:
- Pour lager into a pint glass.
- Create a positive mantra (e.g. you'll be okay).
- Pour a shot worth of whiskey into the pint of lager.
- Either down the contents quickly, or sip while reading a magazine you have lying around.
- Repeat mantra as necessary.

Note: Use whatever lager and whiskey you have on hand. At this point, it doesn't really matter.

There was a time I skipped a job interview, because I panicked that I was under-qualified, but also because my car wouldn't start, so I went back to our house and drank a beer in the kitchen at nine in the morning, while I emailed the company to inform them I had received a position elsewhere, when, really, I was drinking a beer in the kitchen at nine in the morning, wearing the suit your dad bought for me.

Colorado Bulldog

Ingredients:
- 1½ oz Stolichnaya Vodka
- 1 oz Kahlúa Coffee Liqueur
- Cream of choice
- 4 oz Pepsi (Coke if you have to.)

Preparation:
- Combine liquors and cream with ice in cocktail shaker.
- Shake until frothy.
- Top with Pepsi.

When you told me you had a mantra, I asked you what it was.

You told me it was assigned to you by a spiritualist. You told me it was a phrase in Sanskrit. You didn't know what it meant. You didn't understand it. You didn't think it was even translatable. You said you repeated it with your eyes closed in the shower. You said you knew it sounded strange, but it seems to help your anxiety and depression in a way the Lexapro didn't and couldn't. You told me if you said it aloud to anyone else it becomes meaningless.

You said you would tell me, if I really wanted to know.

I then realized I did not love you as much as you loved me.

You wanted to share your inner peace with me, and I just wanted to have another drink at the bar across the street.

Whiskey Sour

Ingredients:

- 2 oz choice of rye whiskey
- 1 oz fresh squeezed lemon juice
- ½ oz simple syrup
- ½ oz egg whites

Preparation:

- Separate egg white from yolk by cracking the shell and transferring the yolk from each half of the shell, draining the egg white into a container below.
- Mix all ingredients into cocktail shaker, without ice, and shake for adequate frothiness.
- Add ice to the shaker and shake again. Hell, shake one more time.
- Strain contents into a highball over fresh ice.
- Garnish with a lemon twist.

> Note: For a New York Sour, float 1 oz of a high-tannin wine (such as a Petite Sirah or a Shiraz) after shaking. This will add a layered effect and add a robustness to an otherwise sweet drink.

I think Brian Wilson is telling me to kill myself.

"What good would living do me?" The sentiment seems pure enough, but hear me out.

I wasn't always the best at loving you. You are doubting it now that the stars are light polluted and, I guess, I made you unsure.

What would I be without you? I always thought it was "do without you" and I don't know the answer to either.

You've left me, other lives are going on (yours), I believe it, but I don't see them (you) in my room between alleys. "What good would living do me?"

I meet all of his qualifications. I'm going to get a bottle of rye, swim in the ocean, and go out like Dennis. What's the point of being heard if nobody is willing to listen?

God doesn't know a goddamn thing, but Brian Wilson seems to.

Rob Roy

Ingredients:
- 3 oz Scotch of choice
- ¾ oz Sweet Vermouth
- Splash of Angostura bitters

Preparation:
- Fill ingredients in a pint glass, fill with ice.
- Stir with a bar spoon, approx. 30 smooth rotations, where the ice moves as one.
- Strain with Hawthorne strainer onto fresh ice in rocks glass, garnish with two Maraschino cherries, no stems and a lemon twist.

The best advice I received from Rob was, "Never forget what you learned the hard way."

Vodka Redbull

Ingredients:
- Vodka
- Redbull

Preparation:
- Combine.
- Drink.

You wake up at noon, though you've been in a jarred state since the construction next door started at 7:30. You get out of bed, put on gym shorts and one of my shirts you took before I left. You walk to your kitchen to leaf through the cabinets, only to find the prospective food unappetizing.

You think about last night, wonder why nobody else was in your bed this morning. You thought you had something going with that boy at the bar where I used to work. He bought you some drinks and talked about the suburbs. He wasn't intelligent, nor that great-looking, but what do you care? You remind yourself: you're single, you're young enough to make mistakes you can later correct. I probably have some boring German girl who I've been following around just to listen to her accent. You think I have forgotten about you by now. You recall how I forgot about you before I left, so now, there is only you.

You turn on the TV and flip through the channels. Nothing good is on. You check your phone for conversations you don't remember. There are more than you thought. The boy who never called back, some of your friends you cried to, and a couple of my friends and former co-workers you slept with. You hope I will find out about them and maybe never come back. Rather than make apologies or amends to them or to me, you continue to stare at whatever infomercial is on. You wait for them to double the offer.

You think about the last time we spoke: a videochat when my parents were in town to take you out to dinner. You waved to me across the ocean, but shot daggers with your eyes. They took you in and you became part of a family you now resented.

You consider going to the gym, but don't see the point. You want people to find you attractive. They will anyway. You consider going for a walk. You need the fresh air, but that would require, you know, going outside, and you just aren't feeling up to it. You go to your room to start cleaning the clutter from your floor. You put on a record. *The Moon and Antarctica*. How did I remember this was your favorite? How could I notice everything about music or a customer's go-to drink, yet I couldn't remember our exact anniversary? To be fair, neither could you. December something. The line from "Perfect Disguise" comes on. "Cause you cocked your head to shoot me down and I don't give a damn about you or this town, no more."

You take the needle off, gently, and pick up the record. You look at the scratches and the dust in the reflection of the vinyl. You inhale, deeply, bring your arm behind your back, and throw the record. It bounces off the wall and onto a pile of clothes, maintaining its composure. Now you're angry, because nothing breaks how you want it to.

Gin Blossom

Ingredients:

- 2 oz Tanqueray Gin
- 1 oz St. Germain Elderflower Liqueur
- 1½ oz grapefruit juice

Preparation:

- Mix ingredients into cocktail shaker. Shake.
- Strain into chilled martini glass.
- Garnish with lemon peel.

We were holding one another in your childhood room surrounded by cardboard boxes labeled "winter clothes," or "art stuff," or "Goodwill." The streetlight outside the window exposed the contours of the sheets on the bed.

"I'd better get going," I said, with my mouth against your hair.

You held me tighter.

I adjusted my chin over your shoulder, ran a hand up your back, rested my fingers at the atlas of your neck. I was overlooking your desk now, the long, shallow drawer left ajar.

You whimpered a sigh. I took us a step closer to the desk, like a waltz.

I could see in the drawer, you had left some paperclips, a few scrawled post-its, illegible in the moonlight, and a couple of number-shaped birthday candles, unburned, a 1 and a 2.

You nuzzled my collarbone.

Had these candles been sitting in this drawer since your twelfth birthday? Maybe your twenty-first? I didn't know you until you were eighteen. I missed your twenty-first birthday, not wanting to make the drive.

I adjusted my hands, backed up to look at your face, but it remained burrowed.

"It's just, I have to work in the morning."

You nodded, your nose rhythmically bumped my chest.

Why would you leave candles? I supposed they weren't "art stuff."

You put your left hand in my right. I rubbed my thumb over the diamond in your ring.

You looked up, our mouths found one another in the dark. You tasted like juniper. We released. I smiled. You didn't.

You let go. You followed me to the entryway and watched as I put my boots on.

"We'll have to meet up soon." I regretted saying 'soon.' I didn't want to say things I didn't mean this time.

Joshua Bohnsack is the author of *Shift Drink* (Spork Press) and *Shivers* (No Rest Press). His work has appeared in *The Rumpus, Hobart, Vol. 1 Brooklyn*, and others. He is an editor for *TriQuarterly* and *Oyez Review*. He grew up on a farm and moved to Chicago.

Long Day Press

New & Forthcoming Titles

Whimsy
Shannon McLeod

Love Stories & Other Love Stories
Justin Brouckaert

The Everys
Cody Lee

On the Campaign Trail
J. Bradley

What's On the Menu?
Chase Griffin

LongDayPress.com   @LongDayPress

CPSIA information can be obtained
at www.ICGtesting.com
Printed in the USA
JSHW030707091020
8626JS00001B/19